# SPEAK UP

## & BE HEARD

Packed with **TIPS** on how to develop **CONFIDENT COMMUNICATION** SKILLS!

**LINDSAY MACLEAN**

Printed in the United Kingdom

First Printing, 2018

ISBN: 978-1-9993365-0-9 (Print)
ISBN: 978-1-9993365-1-6 (eBook)

***ielevate*** Educate
270 Kings Road
Kingston Upon Thames
KT2 5HX

If you want to understand how to build your presence,
present yourself in a more compelling way,
or if you simply find speaking up a challenge,
then this book is for you.

Lindsay x

Lindsay Maclean is a communication and personal development coach. For the last 20 years she has been working with top city institutions, global brands and private clients. She created the ***ielevate*** personal development method in 2006. She works at all levels from 1-1 coaching with senior management to running group training and communication workshops. She coaches individuals to successfully manage interviews, deliver presentations, increase their personal impact and build more significant business relationships. She also delivers a variety of dynamic programmes in schools, in the UK and Europe.

# Contents

# Introduction

# A Very Nervous Child

I look back at my school reports when I was at boarding school in 1988. I was getting good marks, but I was perceived as a "very nervous child".

I wasn't developing as a confident communicator – at all.

When I was at school, I often felt anxious. I would bite my nails and avoid looking people in the eye. I hated being put on the spot and my stomach would feel like a washing machine every time I was asked a question. I generally felt awkward talking to people.

My way of coping with this was to sit at the back of the classroom, hide my face and pretend I was invisible.

My tactic seemed to work well. I became invisible at school, but I found it frustrating hiding myself away because I knew that I could be bold; I knew I had a much bigger personality outside the classroom.

## A teacher decided to try and help me

It was an astute and observant English teacher, Mrs Moore, who, halfway through my secondary school years, noticed that I hadn't ever spoken out. She decided to try and help me.

She took me aside and suggested that I audition for the school play. Ha ha, I thought. Me, audition for a play? What?! Well, I thought, I've got to do something! I hated this fear of speaking up so off I went and auditioned for the play. This took a huge amount of courage for me because I was petrified, but equally I was tired of being branded a nervous child and I was willing to try anything. Not surprisingly, I didn't pass the audition and I didn't get into the play.

A week later, a funny thing happened. A friend of mine who had landed the main part contacted me to tell me they needed someone to play the servant and that she had suggested that I do it. The drama teachers didn't really know me – when you're perceived as a nervous child it's relatively easy to blend into the background, in my experience.

So I agreed to help out and I played the servant in a Charles Dickens school play. I had one line, which was: "I'm sorry ma'am". Amazing.

This was so good for me. I realised that I could actually speak in front of people and I wasn't going to die – alleluia!! After this experience, I would do anything to push myself outside of my comfort zone, and drama, dance and music proved an enormous factor in terms of helping me manage my anxiety and lack of confidence.

The creative subjects I mention – drama, dance and music – certainly helped me build confidence, but I wanted to know how to be myself when I was on the spot, how to express my views clearly, answer questions confidently, put my hand up, and manage difficult people. In short, I really wanted to learn how to be better at communication. However, I didn't learn how to do any of this when I was at school, at sixth form or even at university.

# Leadership training and coaching company – the foundation for my career

After university, my fear and my new-found interest in communication led me to people who could help and I stumbled into a company called Personal Presentation. Initially, I worked in the office where a variety of individuals, from actors to psychotherapists, psychologists and consultants, were employed to teach leaders how to communicate effectively. The difference with this company was that they just taught people how to be the best of themselves rather than try to make them something that they are not.

I struggled to understand why such a critical skill, for which so many organisations are willing to pay enormous fees, was not part of the school curriculum in the UK.

It was becoming very clear to me that communication skills were transformational.

Every day I was gaining more insight into the ingredients needed to communicate well, to inspire and to influence other people. I regularly attended cutting-edge courses related to coaching and personal development training. On top of all of this, I was meandering my way through my own career and using the skills I was learning to become more confident with simply being me and presenting the best of myself. I could see that it wasn't just executive leadership teams in banks and law firms that needed these skills. It was people like me, people who were making the transition from education to the real world of work. And people who struggled to:

- get on the career ladder
- get to the next level with their career
- present data or their ideas
- be assertive with their boss
- get through interviews
- manage difficult people and conversations at work
- feel confident at work
- inspire and influence those around them and above them

While I was at Personal Presentation, I would attend any course at the weekends and in the evenings that was related to career development. This enabled me to co-develop, with my colleagues, dynamic and powerful new development programmes for our clients, aimed at the people below the leaders.

I was discovering that this was an essential skill if you wanted to do well in the business world.

# The catalyst for entering the business world alone

I felt lucky to be enjoying my work and exploring an intriguing new world of communication. Then, out of the blue, I got a call that my mum had suffered from a nervous breakdown and had been taken to hospital. It was a total shock for me; nothing like this had ever happened before. Mum spent several weeks in the hospital and she lost the ability to speak to me and my siblings. It was hard. I adored her, I admired her, and now it seemed I had no connection with her.

She was given medicine that made it even harder for her to communicate and speak up. She became locked in her own thought process and would often stare blankly at us. I could see in her eyes that she had a lot to say but there were no words to go with it, making it hard for anyone to understand. The nurses would spend time trying to elicit words from Mum, trying to get her to speak up. I felt helpless. I cried a lot.

My employers at the time supported me and they would give me days off to visit my mum who was two hours away. One day, I went to visit Mum and I turned around when a familiar voice called my name. It was a teacher from my high school. I hadn't seen her for ten years and it took me a few moments to comprehend that she was in fact a patient, not a visitor. I couldn't believe she was in the hospital too. She offered me comforting words to help me cope with Mum's breakdown and she then went on to tell me her personal story. She had not been able to get out of bed for months or speak to anyone. Now she was beginning to get out of bed, interact and speak with people again.

I remember sitting in the hospital with a lump in my throat, overwhelmed with the realisation that this could happen to anyone at any time.

I sat for a moment and observed the people around me who appeared locked in their own world of thought, and began to realise just how vital communication skills are – for me, for you, for all of us.

So, I thought, not only does learning how to articulate your thoughts and communicate well help you in this competitive professional world, it can also provide a pathway for untangling personal challenges.

It was here in this hospital that I decided to draw on all of the techniques that I had learnt, and was learning, to create a process that would help people communicate their messages in difficult and challenging environments.

So I took the plunge and went out into the world of self-employment. The ***ielevate*** method was born.

The method started as a six-hour programme that focused on how to use practical techniques to help people recreate their best self in a pressurised environment. I quickly established contracts with global firms, in different sectors, and collaborated with many fantastic organisations to help me fulfil this challenge. The programme has evolved but keeps certain principles at the core.

This book shares some insights into these principles and, of course, the personal transformational journey of someone who went from being a nervous child to someone who regularly delivers workshops in front of hundreds of people in schools and high-performing organisations.

# How to Use This Book

In Part One of this book, I reveal and explore areas that form the foundation of my ***ielevate*** communication method: how you communicate messages, the power of energy, story and attitude. Chapters 2, 3 and 4 are where the magic of my work lies. This foundation is key to helping you speak out with more impact.

In Part Two, I reveal specific practical tips on two of the most commonly challenging face-to-face situations – the Interview and the Talk.

Despite the fact that many of us suffer from a fear of social judgment, we are all different, and what might be relevant to you will not be relevant to someone else. Therefore, it's important for you to write down and notice your own thoughts and responses to this book. You'll notice after each chapter the words **"Suggestions and exercises"** and, underneath this, I offer a combination of suggestions and practical actions to take.

So, grab a pen.

I encourage you to read the whole book and then use it as and when you need to dip into it for reminders.

I don't like making false promises, and by no means want to appear boastful, but if you take the time to do the exercises, you'll find speaking up – to anyone – a whole lot easier, and your confidence will naturally grow.

# The Outside-In Approach

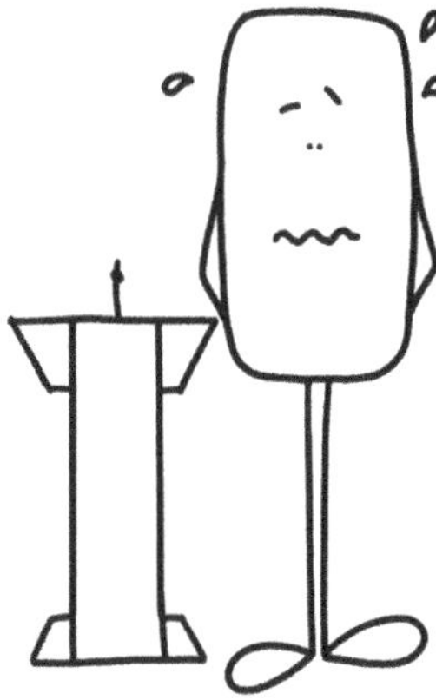

In 2013, *The Times* wrote an article about communication skills. The title was: "Speaking in public is worse than death for most".

I have read many studies, articles and research with similar content, but it's my first-hand experience that has revealed just how universal and great our fear of speaking in public really is. I want to be clear: when I refer to the word "public", this can mean a presentation to 500 people, a meeting with ten, or an interview with just one other person. Some people love delivering large presentations but crumble when they are speaking in a one-to-one meeting or small group.

The problem is that more and more employers are looking to hire a person who can communicate confidently, put their view across effectively, and connect with other people. This is a skill that's a huge challenge for many of us.

So why is it that when one person speaks we sit up and listen, but when someone else speaks, we get bored, and start to think about what we'll be eating for supper?

Most of us know what it feels like when we have been heard, when we've been understood and when we've connected with others. When we connect, and our message lands, we feel satisfied. We feel memorable. We feel listened to and heard.

But a lot of the time the opposite can happen.

When we go into a meeting or have a tricky conversation, we can walk away and worry that we didn't reveal the best of ourselves, didn't say what we wanted to say. The trouble we all face is that, under pressure, we can become self-conscious, try too hard to make an impression, fear what others think and, as a result, our behaviour can change. We can appear arrogant but we're just nervous. We can appear shy and untrustworthy, but we are just apprehensive. We can appear bored, but we are just trying to be professional. Pressure can interfere with our natural ability to communicate well and we can leave people with a dull or distorted version of ourselves.

The good news is you can do something about this.

The ***ielevate*** approach looks at how the outside of you – your behaviour, body language and voice – is affected when you're feeling under pressure. We've all been told we can just will ourselves into being more confident, or just "be ourselves", but it's not enough, you have to take action. I start by looking at how you are communicating your messages and the impression that other people could get. Of course, we all see the world and other people through our own personal viewfinder, and each of us has our own brain and our own experiences; these all shape our attitudes and our opinion of someone.

However, you can be in control, to a certain extent, of how you are perceived by others. Your physical presence, animation, body language, voice and physiology can make a big difference to whether or not you're being heard, taken seriously, or connecting with others. This can have huge consequences for your life outcomes: whether you get the job, get the promotion, win the business or simply feel content with life.

Throughout my work, I thread ideas of how you can work on the inside of you too, but my experience has taught me that you'll achieve far greater results in life and boost how you feel on the inside if you start understanding how to work from the outside in.

Let's explore this…

# Part One

## The Premise and Magic of the ielevate Method

# Chapter 1
## It Begins at School

At school we learn so much, subconsciously and consciously, about communication skills through the way that we interact with friends and teachers.

Of course, we do at home too.

I run workshops for students, teachers and parents. A school will often tell me that it's the parents who influence a child's communication skills. The parents will tell me it's the school. Both environments, along with other factors, impact our communication skills, but I know that school leadership teams who make speaking up a priority alongside exam results, can help the most anxious or shyest child to speak up. I've experienced this myself and observed it through my work.

I specifically remember in one mixed secondary school in North London, I was taken aback by the number of Year 11 students, aged 15 and 16, who confidently put up their hands in class to ask and answer questions – a rare experience for me. I mentioned this to the Head Teacher. She explained that when she had come into the school she had made speaking up a priority. It was noticeably refreshing for me. The students were not scared to ask questions and initiated an exciting and lively debate in the class.

This will most certainly help these students in the professional working environment where communication is vital.

# Teachers and bosses

I have many memories at school of glancing at an expressionless face or listening to a flat voice but not actually hearing anything. Consequently, I would start to draw on my textbook or fidget. This still happens occasionally when I go into a presentation or meeting. I'm not blaming the teacher for my lack of attention. I'm simply stating that some of my teachers were engaging and had everyone's attention and some didn't.

This is often the case at the schools and businesses I visit. There are those that command a room, hold our attention and those who don't. We are in a world where we are inundated with information, so knowing how to command attention and engage others is a vital skill.

# The shiny people

When I was at school, I was always intrigued by the one or two "shiny" students in the classroom who had self-assurance and energy, but the shy ones would always outnumber them. The same shiny students were always willing to speak up, ask questions and confidently answer a question when asked. They were invariably picked to be the team leader, a school prefect or awarded the main part in the school play or music concert. They knew how to speak up. They knew how to shine.

It's clear that this behaviour continues into adulthood.

I always come across the one or two people in my workshops who ask the questions, offer the answers, challenge and speak up confidently right from the start.

The same scenario often happens in the professional world of work. There are those one or two shiny ones, the people who always land the promotions or the best projects.

But you don't have to be the shiny one. My work is about helping you make the impact you want.

I often get asked whether some people are just naturally able to speak up. Certainly some people find it easier than others to speak up, but think of the best teachers, successful lawyers, good actors and artists, sportsmen and women – they all work hard to continually improve their skill. They believe in practice. Watching the football World Cup recently,

I was reminded of the rigorous training process the football players go through for several hours every day to be able to perform on the pitch.

Speaking up requires practice. If you take steps outside your comfort zone and practise, you'll find it a whole lot easier to get great outcomes.

## Asking questions

There is so much you can do.

Learning to ask for help is the first step towards speaking up but this is really hard for many people. I remember it was for me too.

When I was at school, asking the teacher for help didn't enter my thought process until I was really struggling with John Donne poetry in my A-level class one day, and found myself a blubbering mess in my teacher's office.

I was painfully embarrassed to ask anything in front of the class so I spent most of my lessons confused and too scared to ask for clarification.

Anyway, there I was crying tears of frustration and despair, painfully trying to understand what John Donne meant in his poem about a hopping flea. My teacher, Mr Casey, started asking me questions about how I was approaching the task, and he took the time to understand how my brain worked. He then suggested I break the sentences down and use visual maps to help me understand the themes, the main ideas and the detail. He simplified it in my head. He also set me small targets: "Lindsay, put your hand up at least once a week and ask anything." (Oh. Really?) But I did it and quickly realised that it improved everything for me.

I began to regularly communicate with Mr Casey and ask him questions whenever I came across a challenge. I started to realise he was there to support me. A revelation – teachers actually want to help and that's often why they chose a teaching career. It took me six years to work this out. This communication between Mr Casey and me helped me get a good result in A-level English, there is no doubt.

It's interesting how many people I come across in schools who tell me they can't ask for help and consequently feel confused a lot of the time.

Similarly, many people in the business world tell me they don't want to ask for help, in case they come across as incompetent. Or they put expectations and pressure on themselves to know everything. I'll explore this further in the book.

## Asking for help can also break down barriers and perceptions

I remember in one particularly high-achieving girls' school, as soon as the teacher walked out of the room, the students grabbed the opportunity to tell me what a monster she was (sadly, this is not uncommon).

"Really?" I asked. They said that she only seemed interested in giving orders and controlling the crowd. This was their perception. I understood what they meant and I remember having similar thoughts about some of my teachers. Hindsight is a wonderful thing, but I now realise that students also have a responsibility to try and break down these barriers; it's not a one-way process.

So we took a few moments in that classroom to explore how they might do this. One student said, "I could talk to her, describe how I feel in the class." Asking questions and speaking to a teacher or boss about how they can support you will help you to start progressing confidently.

Many of us tend to view teachers and bosses as "different". In fact, they are human beings, no different to you or me.

If you feel scared, unwilling to ask, challenge or put forward your ideas then you may find that you feel confused and frustrated.

The symptoms I experienced at school were the same as what many people tell me when describing social anxiety. But I discovered some wonderful ways of conquering that anxiety around asking questions and speaking up. I made the transition to becoming someone who doesn't get anxious about it and speaks up when and if necessary.

Thinking about any blocks you might have around speaking up is step one of the process. For example, do you have a fear of social judgment? Do you feel you have to be perfect?

More on this later. For now, keep reading if you want to discover some practical approaches to help you speak up more confidently.

# Suggestions and exercises

1. Can you think of that one teacher or boss who inspired/inspires you? What did/do they look and sound like? How did/do they communicate with you?

______________________________________________

______________________________________________

______________________________________________

______________________________________________

______________________________________________

______________________________________________

2. Think about whether you find it easy to ask for help. If not, what stops you?

______________________________________________

______________________________________________

______________________________________________

______________________________________________

______________________________________________

______________________________________________

3. Is there any help that you think you could get in life now? If so, make a note of what kind of help and who you need to ask.

______________________________________________

______________________________________________

______________________________________________

______________________________________________

______________________________________________

______________________________________________

Notes

# Chapter 2
## The Power of Energy

## The how

Many people are convinced that the words they say make a difference. It's not enough.

*How* you speak out, express your views and answer those questions will often make a difference to whether people listen or not. Recently, I came across a wonderfully funny

TEDx talk by Will Stephen on YouTube. His talk is called "How to sound smart in your TEDx talk".

In the talk he wears glasses, he uses both hands to make gestures, he uses PowerPoint graphs and pie charts, he pauses for effect, he changes the pace and tone of his voice and yet he says nothing of any consequence. He begins by saying: "I have absolutely nothing to say and yet through my manner of speaking, I will make it seem like I do." He has the audience completely hooked, laughing and engaged throughout.

Of course content is important, but this is an example of the power of how someone communicates to get people to listen.

## Popular studies

There are many studies that suggest that non-verbals – use of body language, eye contact, facial expressions – dominate conversations.

Dr Albert Mehrabian is Emeritus Professor of Psychology at UCLA, and has become best known for his publications on the importance of verbal and non-verbal communications. In his studies, Mehrabian concludes that there are three elements of any face-to-face communication:

- words
- tone of voice
- non-verbal behaviour (eg facial expressions)

For Mehrabian, non-verbal elements are particularly important for communicating feelings and attitudes. If the words disagree with the tone of voice and non-verbal behaviour, people tend to believe what they see and how they hear it rather than the actual words. For example, if I were to say to a group of people, "I'm really excited to share a new project", how would you expect me to appear? If I looked down and kept my hands firmly by my side, would you actually believe that I was excited? Would you feel excited too? I might simply be feeling self-conscious under pressure, so my body language will tell you that I'm not excited. Chances are that you won't believe I'm excited if you don't see it in me.

There are recognised limitations to Mehrabian's experiments and results. As with most theories, there has been debate and disagreement. However, in 20 years of training, I've witnessed how a person's tone of voice and appearance can make all the difference to a successful result.

In a similar study, American anthropologist Ray Birdwhistell estimated that no more than 30-35% of the social meaning of a conversation or an interaction is carried by the words. Simply put, when speaking, our facial expressions and body language will make a far bigger impact than we realise.

# Put the fuel into how you communicate

So, imagine if you had a smart-looking Ferrari sitting outside on the driveway that never had any petrol in it – it would never go anywhere. It's like you having excellent content and brilliant ideas but not using them. No one will ever see or hear what you have to offer.

Recently I coached a man who had an extraordinary mind. He was a finance manager who hoped to step into a senior management role but kept missing out on the promotion. My first impression of him was that he was shy. He would look away from me while he talked and turn his body to one side. It felt like we couldn't connect and my mind started to wander off when he was talking. I had to keep concentrating and work harder at listening.

The problem is that if you're in an interview or meeting or presentation, you simply don't want people to have to work hard at listening to you, you want them to just listen and hear you.

So, during the course of our coaching journey, we focused on how he presented himself, because this was his greatest challenge. We did several practical exercises and gradually he began to unravel an inner authority. He started to appear and become more confident until he was oozing a personal power which was quite captivating.

I was delighted to hear that he got the promotion next time around.

If you are wondering, "But how? How can I appear and become more confident? How can I find the personal power? How can I improve?" bear with me and read on.

# Your energy

I want to bring your attention to a vital ingredient in *how* you communicate: your energy.

I believe your energy is at the heart of confident communication. When you are energised, you feel good, powerful, inspired, and feel that you can communicate well. Importantly, you come across with conviction and often energise others.

Throughout the day, you generally experience a variety of different energies. If you are going for a job interview, your energy will be different to the type of energy you experience if you are going to visit a friend. If you are going on holiday, your energy might feel different to the type of energy you feel when you are going to work.

Let's have a think about different energies...

## Anxious energy

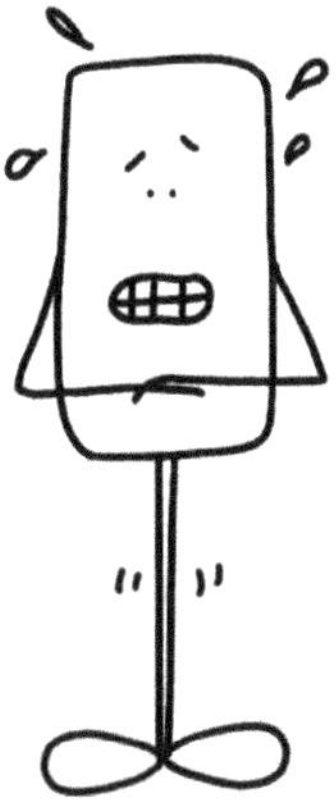

Anxious energy is actually the most common type of energy I come across in people. I believe that we are constantly bombarded with information, which on the one hand has its advantages but, on the other hand, can stir unwanted adrenaline and make us feel anxious. It's great to be able to do business with someone abroad, on email or Skype. It's great to be able to contact people on instant messaging. The downside is that the instant nature of texting and emails might cause anxiety. You may receive an email on your phone when you're having a day off and sitting happily in your garden with a cup of tea, and feel that you have to respond to that person immediately. Often, you don't really need to, but in this world of instant responses and gratification, you feel as though you must reply there and then. This can stir the emotional pot inside and create an anxious energy.

This anxious energy we feel in the body can also be described as the fight-or-flight reflex. We feel things start to happen inside. Physiological changes can include tightening of the muscles and accelerated heartbeat. In my ***ielevate*** workshops, I explore how we can use this anxious energy and turn it into a positive, productive and engaging energy.

I remember delivering a career strategy programme, aiming to support female lawyers transitioning into partnership roles at an international law firm. While we were sitting and waiting for everyone to arrive, I noticed one of the ladies, Martha, who was sitting on her chair nervously at the back of the room and clinging intensely to her mobile phone as if it were helping her to breathe. I went over to say hello. She frantically, anxiously and excitedly told me that her team (who were in the same building upstairs) were attempting to close a major deal that very day. I gave her the option of going upstairs to be part of it or staying for my workshop. She insisted on staying for the workshop, so I briefly emphasised the importance of being as present as possible for the day and asked her if she wouldn't mind putting her phone in her bag. She nervously put her phone away and remained sitting cross-legged, hunched over and visibly tight with anxiety. However, as we began the exercises, Martha started to enjoy herself and to exude a lighter energy. The stern line that was between her eyebrows earlier that day seemed to have disappeared.

When we took a break two hours into the session, the first thing she did was check her phone (most people do). Everything changed in that moment. I saw the shock on her face. She reverted back to the way she had been at the start of the day, visibly turned red and began to draw her shoulders in as she read a disappointing email on her phone. Even though her team were in the building upstairs, she called them from her phone, anxiously firing questions as if it were a family bereavement. It was important to her, of course, and I'm not undermining her job. This just illustrates how often I see the way that instant electronic communication can cause so much anxious energy.

## Transforming anxiety into a positive energy

We continued with our exploration of energy and looked at how to channel nerves. We explored how a positive energy can calm us and help us to feel more powerful. In our afternoon break it was fascinating to see how her call to the team upstairs was completely different this time. It was clear to see how the day had helped her transform her uneasy, anxious energy into a lighter and calmer energy. This seemed to help her work through the challenges she faced and communicate on the phone with her team much less frantically and anxiously.

Anxious energy is so prevalent in today's society. I love the Eastern approaches to managing anxious energy, such as yoga and meditation. I believe that if we consistently weave these into our daily life, our world can become lighter.

Can you describe what someone might look and sound like if they have an anxious energy?

I'm drawing your attention to the different types of energies in all of us, before looking at how you actually turn an anxious energy into a positive energy in practice.

## Happy energy

Think of someone you know with a happy energy. How do you feel when you leave them?

I think Tigger in *Winnie the Pooh* exudes a happy bouncy energy. There are many situations in life that can make us feel happy. However, our response is often key to how we feel. People respond to situations in different ways. Some people would feel happy if it started to snow and others would feel anything but!

Generally, if you've got the job of your dreams, or you're feeling physically fit, or you just won a race, you tend to feel good. Our feelings have a direct impact on the chemistry in our brain that sends positive messages around the body. If you see someone who is happy, you can often see how they display this through their body language. Recently, I watched my son winning a race at school and saw how he punched the air in delight.

A happy energy, like all types of energy, can be infectious. We can find ourselves adapting, responding in a positive way and feeling energised and uplifted when surrounded by this type of energy.

*Notes*

Can you describe what someone might look like if they are happy? Think about their body language and voice.

## Sad energy

Most of us feel sad at some stage in our life. We can be affected by difficulties in our professional and personal world that bring us moments of sadness, or extreme tragic events can leave us feeling low for days. Our body responds to this by feeling heavy. We may hunch our shoulders over and our head tends to drop down naturally. If you find it difficult to come out of this period of sadness, it's important to reach out and seek some help. However, some people continually carry this kind of energy and see the negative in everything, regardless of how good their life may seem. Their outlook on life affects their demeanour, the way they look and come across to others. Going back to my *Winnie the Pooh* reference, I think of Eeyore, the depressive, gloomy grey donkey.

Do you know anyone who reminds you of Eeyore?

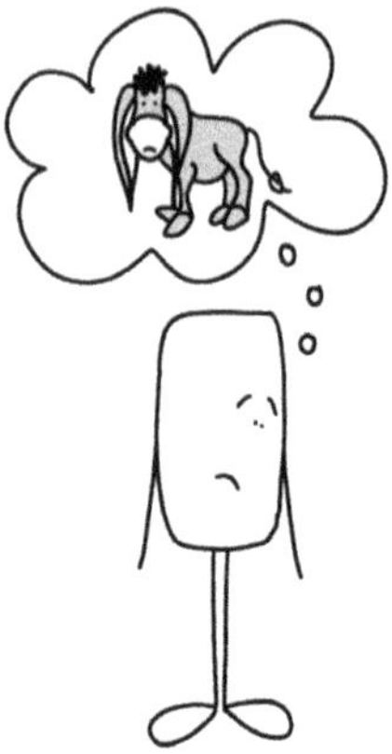

Sometimes, we can give off the impression we're sad just by our body language, especially when we are under pressure.

I remember running a workshop that James, a man in his thirties, attended. He was particularly tall, although his stooped posture and the way he carried himself hid his height. For this particular workshop, at the beginning of the day I asked the audience to present a work project. James stood up, leaned to one side, nervously pulled his sleeves over his hands and began to talk. He spoke of a new project that his department had started working on. He looked down, and his voice naturally sounded sad.

I filmed this and when I showed him the film afterwards, he said, "Wow, I look so morbid and as if I've just been told some terrible news!"

He had no idea that he was projecting such a sad energy to the rest of the world. He said this helped him understand why he often felt misunderstood by other people. With this awareness, and with the help of some practical exercises, he made a few small tweaks. By the time he delivered his final presentation for the day, he felt much better about speaking in public and he was astounded by his own transformation.

*Notes*

How would you describe someone with a sad energy? Think about their body language and voice.

## Spirited energy

This is the energy I believe is buried within all of us, and the type that I believe can help you speak up. Once you know how to unlock your spirited energy, it will make a difference to how you speak and how you connect with others.

Spirited energy is your unique energy that engages other people and allows communication to flow naturally. I think of it as your spirit awakened. No matter if you're an introvert or an extrovert, you can learn to turn it on like a light switch and wrap it around you like a glowing cloak.

By knowing how to use this type of energy, you can avoid people misunderstanding you. If you feel shy, you may come across as cold. If you feel nervous, you could appear incapable of doing a job that you know you are capable of doing. If you learn to unlock your spirited energy and turn that light switch on inside, you'll reveal the best of you and leave little room for misinterpretation.

Imagine you are in an interview and the interviewer asks where you want to be in two years' time. You have prepared as much as possible, but you didn't foresee this one question. We can't prepare for everything. So, you look down and your energy takes a drop. Then you find the answer and feel as if you're bringing yourself back to life. Your interviewer smiles at your response so you feel your energy levels rising again. Things are improving. Things are going well, but right at the end, the interviewer says, "I'm not sure you have the relevant experience." What happens to your energy? It takes a nosedive. You reveal this through your body language and your voice, leaving your interviewer with the wrong impression of you.

In this scenario, someone else has affected your spirit and your energy. This is common in everyday life. If you have no control of when your energy swings between high and low, what does your listener think and feel? Firstly, they might switch off, and secondly they might make incorrect judgments about you.

So our energy can swing between all the states I've explored in this chapter – happy, sad and anxious (and many more I don't touch on here) – but this is not helpful when delivering a presentation or when you're in an interview or meeting.

## Projecting your spirited energy

In order to be memorable and make an impact, we need to know how to unlock, and project, this spirited energy I'm talking about.

When we explore the practical exercises and I ask people in my training room to imagine that they have injected some spirited energy into their system, a common response is:

*"I feel so much lighter communicating my message"*

*"I'm enjoying speaking"*

*"I feel more awake"*

If you feel lighter, more awake and enjoy speaking out, imagine how your listener will feel.

We all know what happens when someone yawns in front of us: we yawn too. Similar idea.

In 1822 Charles Darwin identified that expansiveness among animals equals power. If we see someone opening up rather than closing in, we are more likely to get a sense of power.

You don't need to act, or pretend to be someone you're not, and you don't need to be over the top with your energy, but it's important to increase your energy levels more than you think you need to in order to be memorable. You need to practise, film and watch yourself back to see the impact when you use your spirited energy.

Energy through your body language tells us a lot.

I worked with a musical director who conducted West End musicals, and he said it was only when he filmed himself conducting that he could see how bored he looked. He wasn't bored at all. He loves his work. Once he learnt the importance of revealing and maintaining his spirited energy, he positively changed how he was coming across and how he connected with the orchestra.

I often ask people to tell me what it looks and sounds like when I've asked them to apply spirited energy and watch themselves back. They use words like...

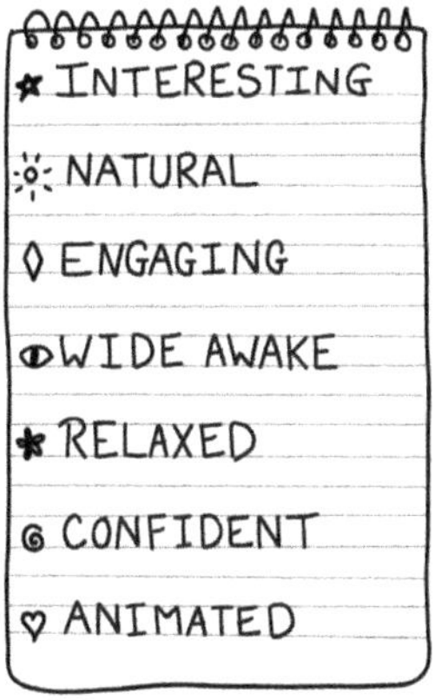


When we haven't consciously switched on our charismatic and dynamic energy we can often sound and look...

A confident, consistent and charismatic energy is key to helping you communicate well.

You can do this naturally by thinking of how you can enhance your natural energy levels. The obvious supporters of a positive energy are exercise and diet. However, as I've explored throughout this book and this chapter, it is often situations in life and other people that can impact on our energy levels. So, first of all, you need to learn how to reveal your spirited energy when you need it the most.

***The important bit – here's how...***

I mentioned turning the light on earlier. So imagine yourself opening up and turning on the light inside you. Imagine you have balloons under your arms. Imagine there's a piece of string attached from your head to the sky.

This will help you to appear more engaging, natural, charismatic and animated.

If you keep practising this, it will eventually become a way of communicating for you. Don't worry about it feeling false when you practise this initially. In fact, it's got to feel strange – you have to learn to do something differently if you want to make a change, and it requires discomfort to begin with, like any learning.

You'll notice that when you do this, your character will become more alive and people will sit up and listen to you more. You have a stronger chance of being heard and memorable in an interview, presentation or meeting.

## Energy in your voice

Most of us include variety in our voice all the time. We use natural pauses when we think of the next thing to say, or to allow the other person to speak; and we emphasise words that we want to highlight. Like a musical score, we vary our tone and pitch.

When we are scared or anxious, we can find it difficult to speak naturally. Our thought process can become blurry or blocked and our voice can become a monotone. We can sound unnatural and start speaking differently. It's important to learn how to bring the spontaneity of natural speech to those pressurised situations in order to come across as real. Pausing and emphasising words play a crucial role and will help you to create that natural musicality in your voice when you are speaking under pressure. If you rush your words and forget to include variety, your listener is less likely to hear you.

## Punctuation and modulation in the spoken word – pause and emphasis

The following two paragraphs are the same. One has punctuation and the other doesn't. Try reading both...

Whenwereadadocumentabookoranemailthereisalways punctuationifnotitmakesitreallydifficultforustoreadand understandafterawhilewegetboredandgenerallystopreading

> When we read a document, a book or an email, there is always punctuation. If not, it makes it really difficult for us

to read and understand. After a while, we get bored and generally, stop reading.

The first paragraph is confusing. This is exactly what it sounds like when we hear someone speaking without modulation. Modulation is the variation in the strength, tone, or pitch of your voice and, for me, represents the punctuation that we can't actually see in the spoken words. I've heard many presentations that sound like one lonnnnnnnnnnggggggg word.

When someone forgets to thread modulation throughout his or her speech, it sounds restricted. It can sound boring, robotic and, most of all, uninspiring.

When you bring variety to the spoken word, you also allow the other person (or people) to process and digest what you've just said – essential for real connection.

When you are speaking under pressure, a simple pause may feel like a lifetime to you, but to your listeners it's normally no more than two seconds – they need this time to digest what you've said, to laugh, to cry, to reflect and to connect.

## Energy in words

It's our intention that can bring energy and conviction to our words. Thinking about your intention before speaking is vital.

For example, if your intention is to have a meeting with a colleague at work about refreshing the development strategies for next year, you need to think about *how* you can communicate that.

Many of us don't spend enough time thinking about our intentions when communicating messages and, in this scenario, you might say something along the lines of...

> *"I think it could be a good idea to urrrm, possibly look at our strategies around development for next year, they might need refreshing, perhaps we could meet if you have time?"*

If you heard it delivered in that way would you think it was important?

But if you heard this...

> *"We need to revisit and refresh our development strategies for next year. When are you free for a meeting?"*

...would you be more inclined to agree to a meeting?

## How does this exploration of energy help?

Tim was an exceptionally talented 35-year-old with an Oxford degree and a strong marketing position in a global organisation. He wanted to be a director but failed to get through the assessments twice because he couldn't connect with the panel of directors interviewing him when he presented.

On our first day I asked him to prepare a presentation based on an idea that would make the company more profitable. He brought his idea to the training session and we sat at the table while he revealed it. I was completely hooked by the idea and found him compelling. I could see how much he naturally brought to the company.

## The perception

I asked him to present the same material to me again, but this time I set up a tripod and video camera and asked him to stand up while he delivered it. Instantly he tilted his head to the side and slicked his shiny black hair to the side. I slowly watched how he replaced his natural warmth and charming energy with a stiff and formal stance. He began to speak, but this time it sounded as if he were reciting a script and he was talking very quickly. I couldn't follow. He appeared to be uncomfortable, making it difficult for me to engage with his content. The natural energy that had flooded out when I kept it informal the first time was suddenly lacking. The very presence of the video camera changed his behaviour and how he came across.

We watched the video together and he quickly realised that in a formal situation he found it impossible to articulate his ideas with the same natural charm that he had revealed when the camera wasn't there.

I see this a lot with my clients and it's easy to blame the fear of the camera, but it's the fear of any formal situation that provokes this uneasy and awkward behaviour that comes out in a person's body language and voice.

## The techniques

This is where we needed to work on the techniques. I asked him to imagine that he had just been injected with a dose of spirited energy, to lift himself up, to imagine he had balloons under his arms. I asked him to imagine the energy flowing freely. I also asked him to think about pausing, and emphasising words where necessary.

We repeated these exercises. He said it felt very unnatural to do this. "Good," I said. "It's got to feel different." If you do what you always do, you'll get the same results. When you learn any new skill you have to do things that don't come naturally. Eventually it becomes effortless.

It clicked. He said learning to unlock and project his spirited energy took pressure off him. He stopped feeling the need to impress and learnt to enjoy what he was saying.

Tim became a director of that company and a year later he set up his own technology company. He credits these techniques, and his commitment to personal development, as being instrumental in his progression.

# Suggestions and exercises

1. If you feel nervous and anxious when you're speaking up, pause, take a deep breath and sit or stand up tall. Put your shoulders back and imagine yourself throwing away all your nerves through your arms and fingers. Shake them out. Direct them towards your audience.

   ______________________________________________

   ______________________________________________

   ______________________________________________

   ______________________________________________

   ______________________________________________

2. Film yourself over and over doing different types of presentations and watch it back. How do you come across? Bored or inspired? Your audience will mirror you.

   ______________________________________________

   ______________________________________________

   ______________________________________________

   ______________________________________________

   ______________________________________________

3. Notice other people's energy around you. Think about what you find appealing. Who makes you feel good and why?

   ______________________________________________

   ______________________________________________

   ______________________________________________

   ______________________________________________

4. Practise unlocking your spirited energy. Remember, imagine you have a string between your head and the ceiling, imagine you've got balloons under your arms when you're speaking.

______________________________________________

______________________________________________

______________________________________________

______________________________________________

______________________________________________

______________________________________________

5. Lift up your voice more than you think you need to. Practise projecting your voice. No need to be over the top but under pressure we often speak more quietly than we think we do.

______________________________________________

______________________________________________

______________________________________________

______________________________________________

______________________________________________

______________________________________________

## Practise. Practise. Practise.

# Notes

# Chapter 3
## The Power of Story

## The story

We are addicted to stories. They have always been a primary form of communication and they are a big part of my work.

Cinema is a globally popular activity and many people are addicted to soap operas – these pull in vast numbers of viewers. People are fascinated by these TV drama series, even though the daily lives and problems of the characters are sometimes not much different to their own. A good story evokes emotion within us. Since the Stone Age, we have been telling stories to teach others, to engage, to create laughter, to inspire and to influence behaviour.

*Notes* What do you see in your mind's eye when you think of a good story?

I think of people. I think of images. I think of colour. I think of a beginning, a middle and an end. I think of anticipation. I think of drama. I think of going on a journey.

## Using stories to help us remember and understand

When I run workshops in schools, I show students how to take lists, facts, figures and key words from their textbooks and turn them into exciting, funny or random stories that they understand. Our brain likes the logical progression of ideas and visual images that comes with a story. More often than not, students are far more likely to remember the story they created on their own, rather than the facts they've been told surrounding geography or history or any subject.

It's easier for them to learn and recall the information if they associate it with what they know, and create pictures in their minds. By coming up with their own story for each topic, using characters and locations they are familiar with, they discover that they naturally become more engaged with the topic.

I recently ran a two-hour parent and child workshop for a Year 11 class and I gave them ten minutes, in pairs, to come up with a story based on the top 20 elements of the periodic table. The only rule was that they had to use each element and keep each one in the correct order of the table. Afterwards I asked for volunteers to come and share their stories.

I saw a number of stretched competitive arms fighting for my attention. I selected two boys right at the back of the room. They came up to the front and faced the group of roughly 60 parents and friends, and proudly began to reveal their story based on the top 20 elements in the periodic table. I remember the story well because it made me laugh and they delivered it with so much energy. I'll just recap on the introduction and how they incorporated the first five elements...

Hydrogen
Helium
Lithium
Beryllium
Boron

"I was sitting down skateboard alley and saw this well fit bird. She was well tall and beaming like the sun (Hydrogen). She was wearing awesome heels (Helium), which I thought was well cool. I asked her if she wanted to come hang out and get down Leafy (Lithium) club and she asked if she could bring her friend Beryl (Beryllium). Beryl was a lovely girl although a bit boring (Boron)."

And so the story went on...

Which are you more likely to remember, a list of the elements or a story like this that incorporates the elements?

## When it's your story, it's far more interesting

The boys were excited and had a lot of fun sharing their story. You could sense the pride they felt while presenting their story to the room full of students and parents. And what's more, at the end of the session when I tested them, they had remembered all the elements in the correct order. While recalling them, they fed back to me afterwards that they had needed their story to remember what came next. Suddenly, they were impressed by their own memory.

Two teachers approached me after the session and said that they had never ever seen those two boys so involved, so engaged and shining like they did during the exercise.

So stories can help you remember information. Also, if it's a story that you have created, from someone else's material, you are likely to feel more confident sharing it.

## Stories help us to be heard by others

By telling a story, rather than delivering a list of facts and figures, you are creating anticipation and painting a picture in your listener's mind. Most of us will often associate more with a story and it can help us to receive and understand messages. I have seen many presentations where I have struggled to read the facts and figures on a PowerPoint slide, or have become lost by the lists of points being made.

A most outstanding presentation that incorporated the story structure well took place at the Rose Theatre in Kingston. The speaker, Rebecca Lowe, had cycled 10,000 miles from London to Tehran and wanted to share her experiences and facts about the Middle East. She spoke for 15 minutes revealing several facts through interesting stories. She described the warm way she was greeted by the locals and the humility amongst the people. She depicted a wonderful culture that was in stark contrast to the negative news of the Middle East that we hear so often through the media.

After the presentation, I had an interesting chat with the man sitting next to me. Greatly impressed by Rebecca Lowe's talk, he told me how his perception of the Middle East had totally changed right there and then. The facts that she revealed about the country had made a real impact on him and he was utterly inspired to face his fear of the Middle East and go and book a holiday. She had completely changed his mind.

Personal stories teach us, inspire and influence us. If Rebecca had just presented a series of facts about Tehran, I don't believe she would have inspired so many of us.

## Stories are a natural way of communicating

You'll often hear children sharing stories; they like to learn through hearing and reading stories. When we enter the adult world (I'm not sure when we make this transition), we are in danger of speaking differently, of losing our identity and forgetting that stories are the most powerful and natural way of communicating.

I've seen many people in meetings and presentations deliver information, but they simply haven't been heard.

If I were to tell you about a recent holiday using a formal tone in a list of bullet points like this...

- I went to Poland.
- I participated in skiing.
- I ate good food.
- There was a lot of snow.

... would you feel excited and want to visit Poland or would you forget about our conversation five minutes later?

I'm far more likely to tell you a particular aspect of the holiday:

> "I went to Poland, the snow was fantastic. On the first day we had a very funny skiing lesson where I went plummeting into the side and covered my leg in bruises while my five-year-old glided casually down the slopes." (This is, in fact, all true.)

Do you see the difference?

The second example is how we speak as humans. It's more interesting. It's natural. The first example is how we approach most business meetings – leaving people bored and uninspired. When we are in work mode, we feel we have to draw on a bullet point structure.

The most inspirational managers, leaders and entrepreneurs I know often thread stories into their meetings and presentations, using simple language to convey messages.

## You can find a story

Sometimes, people make comments such as, "I can't use a story because my presentation is about updates from a recent project and I need to deliver the top line information with clear and sharp points." My response is: why can't you turn updates into a story? After all, the listeners are far more likely to absorb the data.

When I get these types of questions, I push back with my own questions such as, "What do the updates mean to the person you're talking to? Why are they important? Why are they important to you? Why should anyone care about the updates?"

Pushing back on their content often prompts people to unravel their presentation of boring bullet points and begin to naturally reveal an engaging story that makes me sit up and listen – whether it's updates, reports or figures, there is often a story.

## Avoid jargon

Most industries have their own terminology – doctors, lawyers, builders, science teachers – but if someone starts to speak to you using their specific industry vocabulary, do you listen? Do you understand?

Last year, I found myself, on the phone, drifting off while a solicitor was on a roll and spilling out a trail of information I needed to know for purchasing a house in partnership with my brother. I remember hearing "Indemnity contribution" and "Deed of gift". I put down the phone and realised I had stopped listening halfway through the conversation. In fact, I had started to think about what I was going to cook for supper that night and I lost the will to ask any more questions.

We are all in a world where we are overloaded with data, so if someone else is overloading us with words, industry jargon and information, it's easy to start thinking of the next thing.

I decided to try another solicitor. Within five minutes of being on the phone, she told me how she had been divorced and her ex-husband had taken their son to court because they didn't have the right contract in place when the father had given the son a share of the family home. They had made an agreement assuming that as they were a family, the bond of trust would be stronger than any legal issues. They were wrong (which was ironic considering both parents were solicitors). I was horrified by her tale but hooked by her personal story and her professional experience.

So I asked her to send me a contract that would suffice for my particular situation. I read through and asked her anything I didn't understand, and the answer was always delivered in layman's terms, simple English without obscure legalese. I signed up immediately with those solicitors. Her personal story had helped me to connect, trust and truly understand everything I needed to know about my situation.

You might feel uncomfortable going into an interview and feel that you have to reveal all the impressive words you know. Or you might learn some business jargon at work that you think will help you when you present in a meeting. None of this helps your case. In fact, it often has the opposite effect. By adopting language in this way, you're more likely to turn people off rather than impress.

Employers and interviewers want to get an idea of someone's personality. That's why people are rarely hired without a face-to-face interview.

People want to see *you*.

In business using jargon can turn people off. It's difficult to engage with someone who says:

"What tools are in your tool box?"
*I immediately think of my garden shed.*

"What opportunities have you leveraged recently?"
*I immediately picture myself high-jumping – I don't know why!*

"I want to see some blue-sky thinking."
*I can't help finding this phrase irritating!*

"Please contact my VA."
*Erm, who?*

Notes Can you think of any jargon words?

Being human – and being you – will impress someone more than jargon.

## Using "I"

I notice that when people are presenting information, they often use the word "we". This is common in business: people don't like taking responsibility for their own belief or opinion. It's important to define "we" when you choose to use this. Be specific with who "we" means. If you're not giving yourself any status, people like to know who "we" are. Is it a team you work with? Is it a company? Be mindful of this when delivering a presentation.

## People

Don't you find you relate more to a story if you hear about a person or about someone's experiences?

I remember coaching a man who was leading a large team of people in an investment bank. He had had to make several people redundant as part of his job and was facing having to make further redundancies in his team. He told me that morale was so low and that he had been warning people for ages. So I said, "How have you been warning people?" He replied, "They've been coming into meetings twice a month and I talk them through the figures." He felt like he had been advising them to pull their socks up to try to prevent the need for redundancies through revealing a list of poor figures at each meeting.

So I asked him to tell me what redundancy looks like for someone. He described his friend who was left heartbroken and scared without his job. I suggested taking that story into the next meeting, telling his team about the potential impact if they did lose their jobs. So rather than going into his meetings and merely reading out a list of poor figures, he encouraged his employees to think and feel the impact of redundancy through telling these stories. This made a difference to their understanding.

After six months, he told me that his new approach to communication had shifted people's mind-set. They didn't want to be made redundant so, on the whole, they began to find smarter and more efficient ways to approach work. His story structure approach to his presentations was having a positive impact on the business.

## The power of human emotion

At the heart of a good story lies emotion, but it has to be real. It's my belief that emotion is what prompts our decisions. I spoke to a client about this and he said, "But I act on logic. I need to get a job, I need to pay the mortgage and support my family." We explored this idea of logic versus emotion and discovered that all his decisions were actually based on emotion: the reason he went into banking, the reason he sent his children to private school, the reason he needed two cars. This realisation encouraged him to look more deeply at his life and make some changes that have produced happier outcomes.

If we are listening to someone speak and suddenly start to cry or laugh, we are being affected by what they are saying. Somehow, they are influencing how we feel.

A lady called Mariéme Jamme delivered one of the most emotional talks I've heard. After being given up for adoption by her mother in Senegal, Mariéme spent time in an orphanage and 28 foster homes before being trafficked to France, where she grew up in a French underground station. She's now a leading tech entrepreneur and one of the UN's Young Global Leaders.

Through my work I've heard many stories of how people have transitioned from a dark world into a brightly lit one, but none has moved me so much. While delivering her speech, you could hear a pin drop in the auditorium.

I could see that she had taken all 900 people listening to her on her emotional and remarkable journey.

Of course, her story was particularly moving, but I believe there is emotion behind every story. By uncovering and revealing the emotion, you'll build a relationship with the listeners rather than potentially appearing as a robot delivering lines.

## Connecting with others through personal stories

During a group session in the Head Office of one of Global's biggest retail brands, the ten participants told me how inspired they felt, every day, working for the company, even though their wages were lower than the market level. I asked them what made them feel inspired. They all answered, "We love the brand." I asked what they felt made it so special. Interestingly, almost all of them replied with positive comments about the charismatic and inspiring founder of the company. They told me how everyone gets the opportunity within their first three months to have a personal one-to-one lunch with him, and described how he "leaves you feeling overwhelmingly inspired and motivated". They told me that during that lunch he shares many personal and memorable stories. No doubt a part of the company's tremendous success.

# Suggestions and exercises

1. When you're communicating information, think of what story best captures your message and remember to describe rather than explain.

2. Don't be afraid to use "I" when getting your messages across.

3. Try and think of a moment in your life that changed your perspective or taught you a valuable lesson. Create a story, as long or as short as you want. Film yourself and note down how you're coming across. You can do this in front of the mirror.

4. Use your own language; there's no need to speak jargon.

______________________________________________

______________________________________________

______________________________________________

______________________________________________

______________________________________________

______________________________________________

5. Dare to reveal a little more than what's comfortable in your stories. It's ok to be vulnerable, it's real and it will help you to connect with others.

______________________________________________

______________________________________________

______________________________________________

______________________________________________

______________________________________________

______________________________________________

# Notes

# Chapter 4

## The Power of Attitude

My professional experiences and personal journey continue to reveal the vital role of an open-minded attitude. This will undoubtedly help you to improve your ability to communicate and be heard. I reiterate this throughout my programmes.

I'm always greeted by different attitudes when I deliver training and coaching sessions. There are those that make comments like...

- "But things just won't change in this organisation, however much I try."
- "I've tried everything and I'm just really bad at presenting."
- "I'm always getting knock-backs."

... versus those that make comments like...

- "I'm often the one who disagrees with my manager and pushes for change."
- "I haven't learnt how to master a presentation *yet*."
- "I want to learn why I'm getting knock-backs."

Psychologist Carol Dweck, Professor of Psychology at Stanford University, has spent her entire career studying attitude and performance and found that people's core attitudes fall into one of two categories: a "fixed" mind-set (the first three statements above) or a "growth" mind-set (the second three statements above). People with a growth mind-set believe that they can improve with effort; people with a fixed mind-set believe the opposite. Dweck discovered that people with a growth mind-set outperform those with a fixed mind-set, even when they have a lower IQ.

Her study shows that your attitude is a better predictor of your success than your IQ.

From many years of being in classrooms and training rooms, I see that those who find my tasks and exercises challenging but insist on carrying on, often make the most significant transformations.

I remember working with Amber, an accounts assistant for a thriving international retail brand. We had a series of one-to-one coaching sessions booked. Her manager had told me that she was effective in all areas at work apart from her communication skills. However, early on, Amber told me confidentially that she was planning on leaving the company because people "didn't listen to her".

She felt miserable and isolated. I remember, on our first coaching session, she was hunched over, with her arms folded, barely looking me in the eyes, appearing upset and defeated. She had an incredibly negative attitude towards her boss and the company she worked for.

She was candid about her negative attitude towards training and development, failing to see how someone could improve their performance and communication skills through coaching sessions. I knew I had my work cut out. I quickly discovered she had reached the same place in her last two companies – she had got frustrated, she began to see enemies everywhere, developed a negative attitude towards her team and eventually left. She was repeating patterns.

During our first two sessions, it transpired that she didn't like many authority figures (teachers, bosses, anyone above her in a hierarchical system). She viewed these people as arrogant, bossy, snobby or rude. She had a "fixed" attitude towards authority figures. She felt that no one above her would ever listen and she could never change their minds or opinions. This had manifested itself in frustration and an inability to communicate effectively with management.

Throughout the training process, Amber became aware of her attitude towards her superiors and her patterns of behaviour at work. It was as if a light bulb suddenly went on inside her head. She went though a journey of exploration and discovery throughout the coaching, eventually figuring out some simple approaches that would help her to communicate with her boss.

Two weeks after our fourth two-hour session, she wrote to me to say that she had initiated a meeting with her boss and managed to influence and persuade him to change systems at work. She had actually managed to make an impact. This made a huge difference to how she felt about her work and, consequently, she had made a decision to stay in the job. She realised that she was responsible for making change happen. She realised that by changing her attitude to authority, she could get a far greater response and progress more effectively.

Six months later, Amber was promoted into a management position.

Learning how to change your attitude really can make a difference to the way you relate to people, the response you get from others, and how you progress with your career.

# Resilience

Conversations with my grandmother, Doris Miles, who nursed Winston Churchill when he had pneumonia during World War Two, highlighted how an optimistic attitude carried her, and many others, through the war. In her words, "Well, we knew we would win the war and if a bomb dropped, you just got under the patient's bed and then got up again."

I wonder if we would all have the same attitude if bombs were to drop outside our window while we worked? I wonder if we could cope with such adversity? I wonder if we would have such resilience? If we fell, could we just get up again? Could you?

Those who have a growth mind-set understand that failing is a part of life and often see an opportunity in the dark. The optimism my granny demonstrated during World War Two, and that of Sir Winston Churchill, Britain's wartime leader, is a prime example of a growth mind-set.

At school, Churchill had not been considered clever enough to learn Latin and was relegated to the lowest form, which he repeated twice. Rather than seeing himself as a dunce, however, he regarded this as a positive factor in his personal development, for he learnt to love and to understand thoroughly the structure of the English language. He became a prolific writer and, decades later, won the Nobel Prize for Literature.

Others have overcome initial setbacks to achieve spectacular success. Walt Disney was fired from the *Kansas City Star* because he "lacked imagination and had no good ideas". J.K. Rowling received 12 rejections in a row before *Harry Potter and the Philosopher's Stone* was accepted for publication; today her books have sold over 500 million copies worldwide.

Imagine what would have happened if any of these people had given up and let their challenges beat them. Well, many people do let their challenges beat them. However, people with a growth mind-set don't let difficulties paralyse them. This mind-set will help you grow in confidence and confidence will help you speak up.

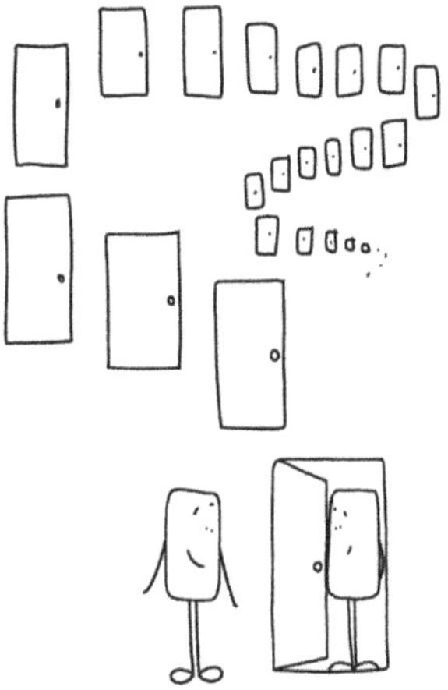

# You're not alone

I remember running a six-hour presentation course with a group of eight people. One of the students sheepishly revealed to me that she had been sent on my course and had nearly phoned in sick because the thought of giving a presentation terrified her and gave her panic attacks (I hear this regularly). So I gently asked her to have a go at facing this fear (as I always do) and attempt a one-minute presentation to the rest of the group, based on a recent project at work. She didn't refuse but as she reluctantly stood up, her face instantly turned bright red; she hunched her shoulders over, became visibly agitated, and began to hastily introduce herself. She then quickly and angrily sat down again, saying, "See, I told you, I'm hopeless." Her voice cracked and her eyes were red and blurry, desperately trying to hold back tears.

I took the attention away from her and moved on to the next person and gave him the same task. He displayed the same physical symptoms as she did: red face, hunching over, fidgeting with his hands. However, the difference with the second student was that he got through to the end of his short presentation. When he had finished I asked him to tell me how he felt. He said, "I hated it, I was petrified speaking in front of people."

(I'm well aware that you might be thinking how terrifying my classes must be! I promise we have fun.)

Two hours later, after some thorough exploration around communication, I ran an exercise that required volunteers to present to the group again, this time using a particular structure I had given them. On this occasion the student who had got angry and teary at the start of the day volunteered to do the task. I asked if she was sure she wanted to, and she assured me she did. She said the realisation that other people in her organisation also got nervous, other people went red, other people felt unconfident when they were put on the spot, had put her fear into perspective and helped her cope.

Needless to say, she got a round of applause as she rose from her seat. She was nervous – very – but she continued to the end, smiling. That was the first step she was taking towards moving into an attitude needed for accomplishing this personal feat. Throughout the day, she continued to put all her energies into the challenging exercises.

Four years later she called me. I was amazed. She asked if I could come and deliver some training and coaching for her team. She had become the Head of Learning and Development for an international company and was managing a large team of people.

When you look around, you'll notice that there are many human beings with similar challenges. You can choose which attitude you adopt: a closed-minded attitude that will keep you fixed in one place or an open-minded attitude that will help you grow.

YOU CAN DO IT.

# Suggestions and exercises

1. Ask yourself if you have a fixed mind-set or a growth mind-set. Do you believe things can be changed or not? Do you believe you can improve or not?

2. When have you been knocked back and how have you responded?

3. In what areas of your life do you need to develop your growth mind-set? For example, do you need to stop saying you have no time for exercise, or no time for hobbies/friends? Have a think.

4. Become more aware of those around you who have a fixed mind-set or a growth mind-set. Think about how you can help them to think differently.

______________________________________________

______________________________________________

______________________________________________

______________________________________________

______________________________________________

______________________________________________

# Notes

# Chapter 5
## Common Barriers

Many things interfere with our natural ability to communicate. Worrying what other people think of us is the most common barrier but I'm going to share the top four that I regularly come across in the training room.

## 1. Technology

I love technology but many people I meet spend so much of their time communicating through electronic mail and text messages that they tell me they have become fearful of face-to-face communication. When we email or text someone, we can edit and delete, we can be in control of our communication. But then we have to go to an interview or we have to present or take part in a meeting. We can't edit or delete anything we might say after it's been said so we become apprehensive of answering questions in case we get it wrong. I regularly hear people say, "I'd much rather email than pick up the phone." Not only can this cause you to become somewhat isolated socially but, I believe, your quality of communication can be diluted. It's a shame to rely on and communicate too much through technology because it's the physical presence of other people – conversations, laughter, and connection – that can nourish us, inspire us and influence us.

# 2. Perfectionism

Over the years I have seen how this thing called "perfectionism" – aiming to be perfect at everything – has destroyed confidence, caused depression and prevented progress. I come across many school students who suffer from perfectionism; they won't speak out unless they are 100% prepared, or they get terribly frustrated if they just get an A grade and not an A* grade. My great-aunt used to say, "If a job's worth doing, it's worth doing badly." I've always remembered her words. By this she meant that if you are always waiting for the perfect situation, you'll never get anything done. And she became a Dame so she must have done something right! This statement gave me permission to get things wrong, and by getting things wrong so often it has helped me get things right.

What's wrong if something is just good or very good?

Why does it have to be perfect?

When I left Personal Presentation to create and sell my own training and development programmes, I remember a friend of mine in a well-known high-performing retail organisation saying, "I've told the Head of Human Resources about your training programmes and she wants a meeting with you." I had only just left the company I worked for, I didn't have a website, I didn't have business cards and I hadn't finalised my plans for the workshops, but I went to that meeting. We had a great chat about what was needed in the company and she signed up over 100 staff for my training programmes. That was just the beginning. I ended up delivering many training and coaching programmes for that company over the years.

I often hear people say, "I need to wait until my website is up," or, "I need to make sure the business strategy is finalised."

I feel we are so conditioned by waiting. Waiting to finish school, waiting to finish college, waiting to finish university, waiting until we feel supremely confident... waiting for retirement. Don't fall into the trap of waiting for the perfect moment. I'm not sure if there ever is one.

# 3. The fear of social judgment

Why do so many of us fear what others think? The quicker you realise that everyone has his or her own opinions and thoughts, the more resilient you'll be to social judgment.

I remember an instance early on in my career, at the age of 27, when I gave a talk at the local business school about the importance of communication. A large room full of approximately 20 white-haired men wearing grey suits greeted me. My one-hour workshop with them, based on communication skills, was part of a six-week business development programme. Colin, the director of the business school, introduced me. I remember seeing smirks, and one man said, "Colin, you always bring us the blonde pretty little things."

I felt as if I'd been stung by a jellyfish.

These types of judgments and comments, made by other people, can make us feel uneasy and uncomfortable. It can change our behaviour and how we feel; we can become self-conscious, vulnerable and start to question our abilities.

But not if we don't let it...

In my experience, this is life, and learning how to manage it as best we can will help us move forward comfortably. I remember at that moment I looked directly at the man who made that remark; I acknowledged in my head that my cheeks might have been pink and ignored the negative words that sailed through my mind. I chose to ignore his judgment of me. I stood tall and cheerfully began my presentation. He actually apologised to me after the presentation.

Always remember, other people's judgments are not about you. This is their issue; it is to do with how they see the world, which everyone views through their own individual lens. As soon as you physically and mentally rise above it and accept that we are all vulnerable to judgment, you can actually start to take yourself more lightly and become almost bullet-proof.

Anyway, on the whole, people are usually too busy worrying about themselves to take that much notice of *you*.

# 4. Our ability to listen

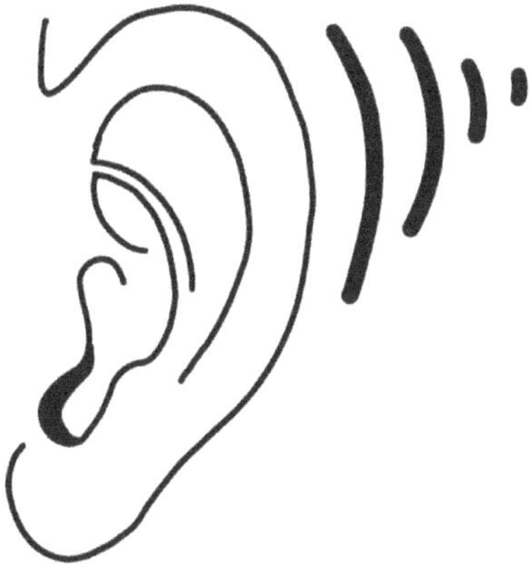

The best words will come out of your mouth when you listen to what others are saying. Listen and hear the question in the interview. Listen and hear your friend talk about her/his problems. Listen and hear feedback that could help you, rather than seeing it as criticism or the end of the world. Listening to others will encourage others to listen to you – most of the time!

# Suggestions and exercises

1. Write down anything that interferes with your natural ability to speak up.

   ______________________________________________

   ______________________________________________

   ______________________________________________

   ______________________________________________

   ______________________________________________

2. Over the next four weeks, reduce emailing and texting as much as you can. Pick up the phone and call someone or arrange a face-to-face meeting. See if you notice any difference at the end of the four weeks.

   ______________________________________________

   ______________________________________________

   ______________________________________________

   ______________________________________________

   ______________________________________________

3. Next time you have a conversation, listen. Really listen and see if you can glean at least three facts from the other person.

   ______________________________________________

   ______________________________________________

   ______________________________________________

   ______________________________________________

   ______________________________________________

   ______________________________________________

Notes

# Part Two

## Where Can You Use All of This?

Tons of tips for the most commonly challenging situations

The Interview and The Talk

So far, I've explored and shared some ideas that lie at the heart of the ***ielevate*** method. The following two chapters look at the most common life situations that require all the ***ielevate*** ingredients – The Interview and The Talk.

At the beginning of the book, I revealed that my approach to development starts by exploring what happens to you on the outside when you're faced with a pressurised situation. Your own awareness and the small tweaks you make will start to produce positive results. It's these positive results that feed confidence on the inside and help you to speak out and dare to be *you*.

I do, however, believe that there are essential things that you can do on the inside to reinforce how confident you feel when you're speaking out. I've touched on this in Part One and I've woven many specific ideas on inside work into the following two chapters.

# Chapter 6

## The Interview

When you go off to an interview, common advice is "just be yourself", but do you find this easy?

More often than not, people find this a challenge and "yourself" can be someone who gets nervous, who over-talks, who over-thinks and who falls apart in an interview.

I have interviewed many people, I have been interviewed and I train people in managing interviews. In this chapter, I'm going to share 20 of my favourite tips.

# The tips

1. If you feel nervous, go for a long walk or run to wake up your body prior to the interview. Get the spirited energy flowing.

2. Just before you enter the interview, go into a private space (it might have to be the lavatory!) and press against a wall really hard. Release and let go. Shake it out. You'll be amazed at how much tension you release.

3. Amy Cuddy delivered a popular TED talk encouraging you to do some power posing before you enter an interview. By this she means tweak your body language – open up, stand tall, lift up your head and get yourself into a powerful position. Her research indicates that, by doing this for two minutes before the interview, you can

increase your testosterone levels and walk in feeling more powerful. Her research, like any research, has been questioned, but I've had several years' experience in this industry and I've seen how this really can make a positive impact. One thing I would say, practise in the mirror some time before the interview so that you don't end up imitating a pumped-up superman or superwoman in the interview!

4. Identify your most energetic and positive friend or family member and speak to them within the 24-hour countdown to your interview. There is often that one person who leaves you feeling energised and positive – avoid energy vampires.

5. Take a few moments by yourself, stand in front of the mirror and imagine what it would be like if you had a light switch inside you that turned off and on. What happens to your facial expressions when you turn it

on? How does this naturally alter your body language? Turn this light on just before the interview.

6. Smile at everyone you meet along the way to the interview, especially the receptionists and security guards – you never know the role they can play in getting you the job, plus smiling will lift your mood.

7. In the lead-up to your interview, take five minutes every day away from everyone and just *be*. Be in the present moment. No screens. Listen to all the sounds around you. Can you hear cars? Can you hear birds? Take in the sounds. This can help to keep your mind calm. Do this just before the interview. It will also help you to learn how to be fully present in the interview, listen and understand the questions.

8. Do your research. Find out all you can about the company and the job role. Look at the website, speak to anyone who works there and read any related news.

9. Brainstorm *why* you are going for the job. *Why* you want the job is really important to any potential employer.

10. Write down the three strengths that you think could help you secure the job and back up each with an example. For instance: "I'm good at developing newcomers and recently designed a mentoring scheme at work that has achieved great results."

11. Take a few moments to visualise walking out of the interview feeling great, punching the air in delight and smiling.

12. Eat well in the lead-up to an interview, including healthy foods such as fruits and vegetables. You'll feel good. You'll look good.

13. Never underestimate the power of breath and its relationship with voice. If your breathing is shallow, it may distort the way you speak. Make sure that you are breathing from the bottom of your stomach to ensure long, smooth breaths. This will help you find your natural voice when you're under pressure. If you're unsure, I'd suggest doing some research on breathing to help you feel calm.

14. Singing is a wonderful way of bringing out the musicality in your voice. By musicality in your voice, I'm referring to the diverse range and pitch. This will help you avoid being the robot with the monotonous voice, so belt out the tunes while you're getting ready for the interview. This also helps you to keep your energy light and lively.

15. When answering a question, think about your *hook* – a short sharp sentence. “I’m good at mentoring people” rather than, “I think that I’m all right at mentoring.” Then follow your hook with an *example*. “I created an award-winning mentoring programme for the graduates in my previous company and helped many people progress in their roles.” Practise answering questions, using this simple structure, with a friend.

16. Dress – make sure you feel good. This is not the time to try out a new look. If you usually wear trousers but decide to wear a dress to an interview, you risk feeling self-conscious. Be you with a touch of smartness!

17. First impressions – always shake hands. Take control rather than be on the back foot.

18. Last impressions – enquire, think of questions you can ask and leave them with a positive upbeat statement, for example, “Thank you, I’ve enjoyed our meeting and I look forward to hearing from you.”

19. Create your own mantra in preparation for any interview and repeat it in your head or out loud as often as

possible. It may be something along the lines of, "I'm committed to doing my very best in this interview," and, "I'm capable of this," and, "I'm worthy of this job."

20. Remember you are interviewing them too. Use the time to find out as much as you can about the role and company.

# Chapter 7

## The Talk

Your main objective is to transfer an idea into the mind of your audience and get people to hear you. I have delivered many challenging talks, and this has been a process that I've had to learn. So here are my top 20 tips.

In my introduction to this book, I referred to *The Times* article claiming that people fear speaking in public more than death. Many people over-think and worry about delivering a talk, so the first five tips below reveal the most common worries and how you can manage them with what I call replacement remedies.

Funnily enough I've been on many training courses and read books where I have been asked to repeat the words, "I am confident," a hundred times a day and then, miraculously, I'm meant to become confident. Mmmm, it hasn't worked for me. But there is no doubt that targeting specific worries and reframing your thoughts can actually make a difference to challenging and scary face-to-face situations.

You'll see what I mean, and how I use replacement remedies here in the following five points about speaking...

## Worries

1. **What if I forget some key points?**

   Create some bullet points/triggers that jog your memory. Avoid scripts. If you do forget, just swiftly move on to what information you can access in your brain. Remember, it's never the end of the world.

   So let's replace the worry with...

   ***If I forget parts, it doesn't matter and I'll manage it. I'll do the best I can.***

2. **They might think I'm stupid**

Take the pressure off thinking about you (we've done a lot of that throughout this book). Focus on your message and why you are delivering a talk. People will always judge you – so what? Let them, it's a part of life.

So let's replace the worry with...

***I'm capable and I'm passing on valuable information.***

3. **I'm worried my mouth will go dry**

This has happened to me several times. It's normal. Have some water next to you. If you don't have water, just pause. A pause to you will feel like ten minutes but will only feel like a few seconds for your audience. I can assure you no one will notice as much as you do.

So let's replace the worry with...

***If my mouth dries up, I'll pause and I won't worry, it's normal.***

4. **I might get a question I can't answer**

So what if you do? Always make sure that you have understood the question. Test out your talk beforehand on people who will ask you questions. You can never totally prepare for questions because you never know what someone will ask. If you struggle to answer, just say, "I don't know the answer to that but I'll see if I can find out."

So let's replace the worry with...

***So what if I can't answer a question, I'll do my very best.***

5. **What if someone knows more than I do?**

There are always people in this world who will know some of the things you know, but unless they are really arrogant, they will more than likely be interested in hearing your views.

So let's replace the worry with...

***There are always people who will know more than me, but I have valuable information to share.***

Use this replacement remedy technique to drown out the negative worries that creep into your head. Say them over and over and over again.

## Now for your intention and idea

6. **Clarify your intention**

   Your number one priority, for any talk, is to clarify your intention. If your intention is clear you will engage your audience. Think about what your intention is for communicating your message. What do you intend your listeners to think, feel and do after your talk?

7. **Clarify your main idea**

   Write the main idea in the middle of the page and create a spider diagram of all the evidence and examples that support that main idea. During planning, add or erase points that don't support the idea. Use Post-it notes, sheets of paper, computer – whatever works for you, but clarify your idea.

## Starting and ending your talk

8. **Connect with your listeners before you start speaking**

   The first few minutes of any talk are critical because you have only a few seconds to grab an audience's attention. Just standing, looking around and engaging with the audience through smiling and your eye contact will help you to establish your presence, gather your thoughts and feel in control.

9. **Opening words**

   Think about your listeners and what they need to know. Do they need to know who you are? Do they need you to clarify expectations for the talk? Do you need to let them know what time they can get away? If they don't have this information, they will want you to give it to them. Use your imagination here. Think about what will grab their attention immediately: a story, a question, a quote, a fact, a joke – think about what will hook them.

10. **Ending your talk**

    Think about what you want your listeners to take away. Do you want them to do something after your talk, for example support a good cause, or sign up to an online programme? Do you want to leave them laughing? I often end with a story or a quotation that illustrates my point, a surprising fact or a call to action. Remember, always say thank you to your listeners.

## The delivery

**11. Make your talk conversational**

My favourite tip. An audience will respond far better when you take a relaxed and natural conversational approach to presenting. Imagine you're telling a friend.

**12. Examples and analogies**

Examples and analogies can help you clarify your points and unfamiliar concepts. They bring the subject to life, adding perspective and depth. If you are giving a talk on climate change and say, "Climate change will affect us in the future," then you have a valuable and interesting point, but if you can offer a specific example of the impact of climate change, you'll help your listeners to fully understand.

**13. Nerves**

Nerves are a part of us. There is no magic wand to get rid of them, but they can actually be incredibly useful. The most famous presenters, sportsmen and public figures get nervous. Your nerves are important, and in Part One of this book, I suggested how you can transform them into a positive and spirited energy.

14. **Vocal and physical fidgeting**

Avoid sloppy colloquialisms, particularly “like” and “you know”. Try not to pepper your pauses with “er” and “um”. Don’t fiddle with your hair, your jewellery, your watch or the change in your pocket. Such unconscious behaviours can detract from your presentation. Video a practice run-through of your talk so that you can check whether you are doing any of these.

15. **Present *you*, not a PowerPoint**

People always want to hear from the human being. I don’t use PowerPoint slides unless I have to show people something to amplify my point. Someone once told me that PowerPoint takes the power out of the point. This, I believe, is so true.

16. **Speak with conviction**

    You know what it sounds like when you hear someone who doubts themselves? Say it like you mean it. Practise, practise, practise.

17. **Emphasis**

    Emphasise key words. There is a difference between "I *want* to take you and your friends out" and "I want to take *you* and your friends out". Be sure to use emphasis straight after a pause to bring your listeners back in again.

18. **Recovery – when things go wrong**

    Don't rely on technology. Only use technology when you really have to for back-up. I've seen too many talks where the technology has failed and the presenter has found it difficult to cope. If you stumble over your words, catch yourself speaking quickly or forget your thread, then pause, *breathe* and slowly repeat what you were trying to say.

19. **Eye contact**

    Never underestimate the power of eye contact. By looking people in the eye, you gain trust and build connection.

20. **Pause**

I've mentioned this a lot because it has many advantages. When you pause throughout a talk, you give yourself time to think and choose the next words or phrase. You also allow people to think about your points and follow your journey. We often feel like we have to keep going when we are under pressure – we really don't.

# Chapter 8
## Conclusion

In most schools, there is currently no specific lesson for learning how to speak up confidently, yet in the business world the requirement for this skill is tremendous. Employers often tell me they are looking for candidates who can work with a wide variety of people, build and expand a network and work collaboratively in a team.

So this, put simply, is about being able to communicate and connect with other people.

The skills that I learnt have helped me to be assertive, helped me put up my hand even though my face was bright pink, helped me speak up in meetings, helped me to be in the moment and to feel present when I'm communicating under pressure.

Today I gave a presentation to 300 students and I loved it. I didn't over-prepare. I didn't let the nerves swallow me up. I focused on what they wanted to hear from me and enjoyed myself immensely. I've learnt how to do it now and it feels really good.

Most of all, learning about how to speak up has helped me manage the most challenging times of my life. When I lost my mum, my ability to speak up with friends, family and strangers nourished me and helped me to unravel the complex feelings of sadness. If I had remained that very nervous child who never spoke up, I wonder how I would have coped.

So, please practice using *your* voice, hearing what others tell you, unlocking your spirited energy and sharing *your* stories. You'll find speaking up can eventually become easier and you will feel lighter.

Good luck. I'd love to know how you get on, feel free to contact me at www.ielevate.co.uk.

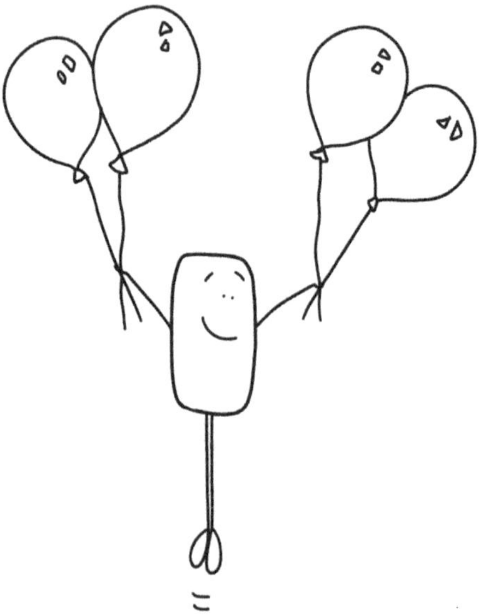

# Thank You

Thank you to my magnificent friends and family for helping me with this book. An extra-special thanks to Jill. Thanks to the team at Librotas. Thank you to Ellie for the illustrations and a whole lot more.

Thank you to the many people who have attended my workshops and shared their stories to make this book possible.

*This book was Inspired by my mum and*
*I hope it inspires my son, Sam.*

Lightning Source UK Ltd.
Milton Keynes UK
UKHW022109290319
340140UK00009B/282/P

9 781999 336509